Fun Food for Cool Cooks

Cheesecake Cupcakes

AND OTHER CAKE RECIPES

by Brekka Hervey Larrew

Capstone press

Mankato, Minnesota

Snap Books are published by Capstone Press,
151 Good Counsel Drive, P.O. Box 669, Mankato, Minnesota 56002.
www.capstonepress.com

Library of Congress Cataloging-in-Publication Data
Larrew, Brekka Hervey.
  Cheesecake cupcakes and other cake recipes / by Brekka Hervey Larrew.
  p. cm. — (Snap books. Fun food for cool cooks)
  Summary: "Provides fun and unique recipes for cakes including cheesecake cupcakes,
gooey apple dump cake, and cookies and cream cake. Includes easy instructions and a helpful tools glossary
with photos" — Provided by publisher.
  Includes bibliographical references and index.
  ISBN-13: 978-1-4296-2016-1 (hardcover)
  ISBN-10: 1-4296-2016-1 (hardcover)
  1. Cake — Juvenile literature. I. Title. II. Series.
TX771.L347 2009
641.8'653 — dc22   2008001761

Editor: Kathryn Clay
Designer: Juliette Peters
Photo Stylist: Sarah L. Schuette

Photo Credits:
All principle photography in this book by Capstone Press/Karon Dubke
Capstone Press/TJ Thoraldson Digital Photography, cooking utensils (all)
David Larrew, 32

PAGE 8

PAGE 14

PAGE 18

PAGE 22

PAGE 24

PAGE 26

TABLE OF CONTENTS

INTRODUCTION

SEEING STARS

When choosing a recipe, let the stars be your guide! Just follow this chart to find recipes that fit your cooking comfort level.

EASY: ★ ☆ ☆
MEDIUM: ★ ★ ☆
ADVANCED: ★ ★ ★

Cakes are great for birthdays. They're also good for celebrating an A+ on your math test. You could even whip up a cake for the school bake sale. Because cakes are tasty and fun to make, you can bake a cake just about any time.

Do you prefer fruity flavors or chocolate? Are you hungry for something light or something rich? Whatever you're craving, you can find a cake recipe in this book that will satisfy your taste buds.

METRIC CONVERSION GUIDE

United States	Metric
¼ teaspoon	1.2 mL
½ teaspoon	2.5 mL
1 teaspoon	5 mL
1 tablespoon	15 mL
¼ cup	60 mL
⅓ cup	80 mL
½ cup	120 mL
⅔ cup	160 mL
¾ cup	175 mL
1 cup	240 mL
1 quart	1 liter

1 ounce	30 grams
2 ounces	55 grams
4 ounces	110 grams
½ pound	225 grams
1 pound	455 grams

Fahrenheit	Celsius
325°	160°
350°	180°
375°	190°
400°	200°
425°	220°
450°	230°

All good cooks know that a successful recipe takes a little preparation. Use this handy checklist to save time when working in the kitchen.

BEFORE YOU BEGIN

READ YOUR RECIPE

Once you've chosen a recipe, carefully read over it. Everything will go smoothly if you understand the steps and skills.

CHECK THE PANTRY

Make sure you have all the ingredients on hand. After all, it's hard to bake cookies without sugar!

DRESS FOR SUCCESS

Wear an apron to keep your clothes clean. Roll up long sleeves. Tie long hair back so it doesn't get in your way — or in the food.

GET OUT YOUR TOOLS

Sort through the cupboards and gather all the tools you'll need to prepare the recipe. Can't tell a spatula from a mixing spoon? No problem. Refer to the handy tools glossary in this book.

PREPARE YOUR INGREDIENTS

A little prep time at the start will pay off in the end.

- Rinse any fresh ingredients such as fruit and vegetables.
- Use a peeler to remove the peel from foods like apples and carrots.
- Cut up fresh ingredients as called for in the recipe. Keep an adult nearby when using a knife to cut or chop food.
- Measure all the ingredients and place them in separate bowls or containers so they're ready to use. Remember to use the correct measuring cups for dry and wet ingredients.

PREHEAT THE OVEN

If you're baking treats, it's important to preheat the oven. Cakes, cookies, and breads bake better in an oven that's heated to the correct temperature.

The kitchen may be unfamiliar turf for many young chefs. Here's a list of trusty tips to help you keep safe in the kitchen.

KITCHEN SAFETY

ADULT HELPERS

Ask an adult to help. Whether you're chopping, mixing, or baking, you'll want an adult nearby to lend a hand or answer questions.

FIRST AID

Keep a first aid kit handy in the kitchen, just in case you have an accident. A basic first aid kit contains bandages, a cream or spray to treat burns, alcohol wipes, gauze, and a small scissors.

WASH UP

Before starting any recipe, be sure to wash your hands. Wash your hands again after working with messy ingredients like jelly or syrup.

HANDLE HABITS

Turn handles of cooking pots toward the center of the stove. You don't want anyone to bump into a handle that's sticking off the stove.

USING KNIVES

It's always best to get an adult's help when using knives. Choose a knife that's the right size for your hands and the food. Hold the handle firmly when cutting, and keep your fingers away from the blade.

COVER UP

Always wear oven mitts or use pot holders to take hot trays and pans out of the oven.

KEEP IT CLEAN

Spills and drips are bound to happen in the kitchen. Wipe up messes with a paper towel or clean kitchen towel to keep your workspace tidy.

People have been making cheesecakes for thousands of years. With a creamy filling and crumbly crust, it's no surprise that cheesecake is still a favorite dessert.

DIFFICULTY LEVEL: ★ ★ ☆
MAKES: 12 CUPCAKES
PREHEAT OVEN: 350° FAHRENHEIT

CHEESECAKE CUPCAKES

WHAT YOU NEED

Ingredients

5 tablespoons butter, softened
1 cup graham cracker crumbs
1 teaspoon cinnamon
½ tablespoon sugar
1 (8-ounce) package cream cheese, softened
½ cup sugar
1 teaspoon vanilla extract
2 eggs
1 (21-ounce) can cherry pie filling

Tools

2 small bowls

pastry blender

baking cups

muffin pan

mixing bowl

electric mixer

rubber scraper

oven mitt   pot holder

1 To make the crust, place butter in a small bowl. Add graham cracker crumbs, cinnamon, and ½ tablespoon sugar. Use a pastry blender or large fork to mix these ingredients together.

2 Put baking cups into a muffin pan. Press 1 tablespoon of the crust firmly into the bottom of each cup.

3 In a mixing bowl, add cream cheese, ½ cup sugar, and vanilla. Mix ingredients together with an electric mixer on low speed for 2 minutes.

4 Crack eggs into a second small bowl and throw away shells. Add eggs to the mixing bowl. Mix on high for 3 minutes. Stop several times to scrape the sides and bottom of the bowl with a rubber scraper.

5 Fill each baking cup ¾ full of batter. Bake for 25 minutes or until cracks start forming on the cupcakes. Turn the oven off and crack the oven door open. Leave cupcakes in the oven for 10 minutes.

6 Use oven mitts or pot holders to remove pan from the oven. Refrigerate for 1 hour. Top each cupcake with cherry pie filling.

Make it a Cake

With a spring-form pan, you can bake this recipe as a whole cheesecake. Just double each ingredient. First, spread the graham cracker crust over the bottom of the pan. Then, pour the batter on top. Bake at 350° Fahrenheit for 50 minutes or until cracks start to form on top of the cheesecake. Turn the oven off and crack the oven door open. Leave cake in the oven for 10 minutes. Refrigerate at least 1 hour before adding pie filling.

You know peanut butter tastes great on sandwiches and in cookies. But it's also great in cake. Mix the peanut butter with chocolate, and you've got a hit that's sure to please.

DIFFICULTY LEVEL: ★ ★ ☆
MAKES: 1 BUNDT CAKE
PREHEAT OVEN: 350° FAHRENHEIT

PEANUT BUTTER CAKE

WHAT YOU NEED

●● *Ingredients*

2 cups flour
2 cups brown sugar, firmly packed
1 cup creamy peanut butter
½ cup (1 stick) butter, softened
3 eggs
1 teaspoon baking powder
1 cup milk
1 teaspoon vanilla extract
1 bottle peanut butter ice cream topping
1 bottle fudge ice cream topping

●● *Tools*

mixing bowl

electric mixer

small bowl

rubber scraper

Bundt pan

oven mitt

nonstick cooking spray

pot holder

1 In a mixing bowl, combine flour, brown sugar, peanut butter, and butter. Use an electric mixer on medium speed to mix ingredients. Mix until the ingredients form a crumb-like texture.

2 Break eggs into a small bowl and throw away shells. Add eggs, baking powder, milk, and vanilla to the mixing bowl. Beat on low speed until the mixture is moist. Beat an additional 4 minutes on medium speed. Use a rubber scraper to remove batter from side of bowl.

3 Spray a Bundt pan with nonstick cooking spray. Pour batter into the pan. Bake for 40–45 minutes.

4 Use oven mitts or pot holders to remove pan from the oven. Cool for 1 hour.

5 When cake has cooled, drizzle peanut butter topping and fudge topping over the cake.

Tasty Tips

Add more chocolate flavor by stirring 1 cup chocolate chips into the batter before baking. If you don't have a Bundt pan, you can use a 9 x 13 baking pan.

Bundt Background

Bundt pans were first created in 1950. People used these pans to make German coffee cakes. In 1966, a Bundt cake recipe won second place in a Pillsbury baking contest. Since then, more than 50 million Bundt pans have been sold worldwide.

Leaves are falling and temperatures are dropping. Fall is the perfect time to make a hearty apple cake. With this dump cake, you just put ingredients right into the pan. What's easier than that?

DIFFICULTY LEVEL: ★ ☆ ☆
MAKES: 1 (9 X 13) CAKE
PREHEAT OVEN: 350° FAHRENHEIT

GOOEY APPLE DUMP CAKE

WHAT YOU NEED

•• *Ingredients*

2 (21-ounce) cans apple pie filling
1 teaspoon cinnamon
1 teaspoon nutmeg
1 teaspoon allspice
¼ teaspoon ground cloves
2 tablespoons sugar
1 (18-ounce) box spice cake mix
¾ cup (1½ sticks) butter
1 cup chopped walnuts
¼ cup powdered sugar

•• *Tools*

9 x 13 baking pan

rubber scraper

small bowl

microwave-safe bowl

oven mitt

pot holder

1 Pour both cans of apple pie filling into a 9 x 13 baking pan. Spread out pie filling with a rubber scraper.

2 In a small bowl, mix cinnamon, nutmeg, allspice, cloves, and sugar. Sprinkle mixture over the apple pie filling.

3 Sprinkle dry cake mix over the spiced apples.

4 In a microwave-safe bowl, microwave butter until melted, about 30 seconds. Pour melted butter evenly over cake mix. Sprinkle walnuts on top.

5 Bake for 50–60 minutes or until brown on top and bubbly along the sides.

6 Use oven mitts or pot holders to remove pan from the oven. Sprinkle powdered sugar over cake. Serve warm.

13

Not Nuts about Nuts?

If you're not a fan of walnuts, you can still make a crunchy topping for this cake. Just substitute granola for the walnuts.

Need a sweet way to end a summer picnic or backyard barbeque? Serve guests Very Berry Shortcakes. Filled with juicy strawberries and fresh blueberries, this cake makes a great summertime treat.

DIFFICULTY LEVEL: ★ ★ ☆
MAKES: 8 SHORTCAKES
PREHEAT OVEN: 425° FAHRENHEIT

VERY BERRY SHORTCAKE

WHAT YOU NEED

•• *Ingredients*

2 cups fresh strawberries
1 cup fresh blueberries
¼ cup sugar
1½ cups flour
2 teaspoons baking powder
¼ teaspoon salt
2 tablespoons sugar
6 tablespoons butter
⅔ cup heavy cream
1 tablespoon honey
1 (12-ounce) container whipped topping
8 strawberries, whole

•• *Tools*

cutting board   paring knife   small bowl

mixing bowl   pastry blender   rubber scraper

baking sheet   tablespoon   oven mitt

nonstick cooking spray

pot holder   serrated knife

1 On a cutting board, use a paring knife to cut strawberries into small pieces. Put strawberry pieces in a small bowl. Add blueberries and ¼ cup sugar to the small bowl and set aside.

2 In a mixing bowl, add flour, baking powder, salt, 2 tablespoons sugar, and butter. Blend ingredients together with a pastry blender or large fork.

3 Add cream and honey to the mixing bowl. Use a rubber scraper to form mixture into a ball.

4 Spray a baking sheet with nonstick cooking spray. Drop spoonfuls of dough on the baking sheet, about 2 inches apart. Bake for 10–12 minutes.

5 Use oven mitts or pot holders to remove baking sheet from the oven. When biscuits have cooled, use a serrated knife to cut the biscuits in half.

6 Place ¼ cup berry mixture and 2 tablespoons whipped topping on the bottom half of biscuits. Cover with the top half. Top each biscuit with 2 tablespoons whipped topping and a strawberry.

14

A Tasty Tradition

You may have eaten strawberry shortcake made with sponge cake or angel food cake. This is different from traditional shortcakes made in Europe. Traditional shortcake tastes like a biscuit. It is made with butter or shortening to make the cake more crumbly. In the 1850s, Americans began adding strawberries to their shortcake. Soon, an American tradition was born.

15

Bring the outside in with this beautiful garden cake. Coconut grass, graham cracker dirt, and gumdrop flowers make this chocolate pound cake colorful and delicious.

DIFFICULTY LEVEL: ★ ★ ★
MAKES: 1 (9 X 5) CAKE
PREHEAT OVEN: 350° FAHRENHEIT

FLOWERS IN THE GARDEN CAKE

WHAT YOU NEED

●● *Ingredients*

2 eggs
1 (16-ounce) box pound cake mix
⅓ cup cocoa powder
¾ cup milk
½ cup shredded coconut
green food coloring
1 (16-ounce) can chocolate frosting
½ cup chocolate graham cracker crumbs
10 large gumdrops
10 standard green gumdrops

●● *Tools*

mixing bowl

electric mixer

loaf pan

small bowl

wooden spoon

oven mitt

pot holder

serrated knife

rolling mat

rolling pin

nonstick cooking spray
large plate
mini cookie cutter
10 toothpicks

1 Break eggs into a mixing bowl and throw away shells. Add cake mix, cocoa, and milk to eggs. Mix with an electric mixer on low speed for 30 seconds. Mix for 3 minutes on medium speed.

2 Spray a loaf pan with nonstick cooking spray. Pour batter into the pan. Bake for 60 minutes.

3 While cake is baking, put coconut into a small bowl. Add a few drops of food coloring. Stir with a wooden spoon until coconut turns green.

4 Use oven mitts or pot holders to remove pan from oven. Allow cake to cool for 1 hour.

5 Put cake on a large plate. With a serrated knife, slice a thin layer off top of cake so cake is flat. Frost top and sides of cake. Spread chocolate graham cracker crumbs on top of cake. Cover sides with coconut.

6 On a rolling mat, flatten large gumdrops with a rolling pin. Use a mini cookie cutter to cut the gumdrops into flowers. Poke toothpicks into the flowers and arrange on cake. Spread green gumdrops around cake to look like leaves.

That's One Heavy Cake

Pound cake is named for the ingredients used to make it. Traditional pound cake recipes used one pound each of butter, flour, sugar, and eggs. The cake was popular because people could easily remember the ingredients. Now, pound cakes are usually made with smaller amounts of these ingredients. This keeps the cakes from being too heavy.

This cake is perfect for anyone who loves chocolate. It combines light chocolate cake, rich chocolate frosting, and yummy chocolate chips! Plus, the cake is so soft it almost melts in your mouth.

DIFFICULTY LEVEL: ★ ★ ★
MAKES: 1 (9 X 9) CAKE
PREHEAT OVEN: 375° FAHRENHEIT

TRIPLE CHOCOLATE CAKE

WHAT YOU NEED

•• Ingredients

1 cup (2 sticks) butter
1 cup buttermilk
¼ cup cocoa powder
2 cups flour
2 cups sugar
¼ teaspoon salt
2 eggs
1 cup plain yogurt
1½ teaspoons soda
1 (16-ounce) can fudge frosting
¼ cup chocolate chips

•• Tools

saucepan   wooden spoon   small bowl

whisk   2 cake pans   oven mitt

nonstick cooking spray

pot holder

1 Place butter into a saucepan. Add buttermilk and cocoa. Heat mixture on high until boiling, about 5 minutes. Use a wooden spoon to stir mixture as it heats. Remove saucepan from the heat. Let mixture cool for 30 minutes.

2 When cocoa mixture has cooled, add flour, sugar, and salt to the saucepan. Stir ingredients together with the wooden spoon.

3 Crack eggs into a small bowl and throw away shells. Add eggs, yogurt, and baking soda to the saucepan. Beat ingredients with a whisk until batter is smooth.

4 Spray baking pans evenly with nonstick cooking spray. Pour batter into the cake pans (square or round). Bake for 25–30 minutes.

5 Use oven mitts or pot holders to remove cake pans from the oven. Allow cakes to cool for 1 hour.

6 Spread fudge frosting on top of one cake. Place the other cake on top of the frosted cake. Cover sides and top of cake with frosting. Sprinkle chocolate chips on top.

Heat It Up

To dissolve a solid substance in a liquid, just heat it up. Heat helps most substances dissolve faster and better. Without adding heat, you would have to stir for a long time to get your cocoa to dissolve. And you might end up with lumps of cocoa in your cake.

This cake looks fluffy like a cloud, and it is full of colors like a rainbow. It makes a delicious centerpiece at any party.

RAINBOW ANGEL FOOD CAKE

WHAT YOU NEED

●● *Ingredients*

1 (16-ounce) box angel food cake mix
1¼ cups cold water
4-5 drops red food coloring
4-5 drops yellow food coloring
4-5 drops blue food coloring
1 (14-ounce) package shredded coconut
⅔ cup powdered sugar
2 tablespoons butter, melted
2 tablespoons lemon juice

●● *Tools*

mixing bowl

electric mixer

4 small bowls

angel food cake pan

rubber scraper

oven mitt

pot holder

wire cooling rack

cutting board

serrated knife

whisk

parchment paper
2 plates

1 In a mixing bowl, add cake mix and water. With an electric mixer, mix on low speed for 1 minute. Beat another minute on medium speed.

2 Pour batter into three small bowls. Mix red food coloring into one bowl. Mix yellow food coloring into another bowl. Mix blue food coloring into a third bowl.

3 Line bottom of the pan with parchment paper. Spread red batter in the bottom of the cake pan with a rubber scraper. Spread yellow and blue batter over the red batter. Bake on the lowest oven rack for 40–45 minutes or until the cake's top is brown and cracked.

4 Use oven mitts or pot holders to remove cake pan from the oven. Turn cake upside down on a wire cooling rack. Allow cake to cool for 1 hour.

5 Place cake on a cutting board. Cut cake in half with a serrated knife. Spread coconut out over two plates. Stand each cake half on a plate.

6 In a small bowl, use a whisk to combine powdered sugar, melted butter, and lemon juice. Drizzle glaze over cakes.

Climbing Cake

You don't need to grease the pan when making angel food cake. This cake doesn't use baking powder or baking soda to rise. Instead, the batter climbs up the sides of the pan as the cake bakes. If you greased the pan, the sides would become slippery. Then the cake wouldn't be able to climb. You would end up with a flat, sticky mess instead of a light, fluffy cake.

Can't decide between a cookie or a slice of cake?
Now you can have both. There's a hidden layer of cookies
that creates a sweet surprise when this cake is cut.

DIFFICULTY LEVEL: ★ ★ ★
MAKES: 1 (9 X 13) CAKE
PREHEAT OVEN: 350° FAHRENHEIT

COOKIES AND CREAM CAKE

WHAT YOU NEED

•• Ingredients

½ cup shortening
1½ cups sugar
2 cups flour
1 tablespoon baking powder
½ teaspoon salt
1 cup milk
4 egg whites
½ tablespoon vanilla
1 package chocolate sandwich cookies
1 (16-ounce) can cream cheese frosting

••Tools

mixing bowl   rubber scraper   electric mixer

  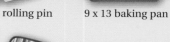

small bowl   rolling pin   9 x 13 baking pan

zip-top plastic bag
nonstick cooking spray

oven mitt   pot holder

1 In a mixing bowl, cream together shortening and sugar with a rubber scraper.

2 Add flour, baking powder, salt, and milk to the mixing bowl. Mix ingredients with an electric mixer on low speed for 1 minute. Mix 2 minutes on medium speed.

3 In a small bowl, separate egg whites. (See Trusty Tip.) Add egg whites and vanilla to the mixing bowl and beat with the mixer for 2–3 minutes.

4 Place 10 sandwich cookies in a zip-top plastic bag. Gently smash bag with a rolling pin until the cookies are crumbled. Stir crumbled cookies into batter with the rubber scraper.

5 Spray a 9 x 13 baking pan with nonstick cooking spray. Pour half of the batter into the cake pan. Spread 18 whole sandwich cookies over the batter. Cover with remaining batter. Bake for 30–35 minutes.

6 Use oven mitts or pot holders to remove cake pan from the oven. Allow cake to cool for 1 hour. Frost the cake. Crumble 5 sandwich cookies and sprinkle on top of the frosting.

In a Hurry?

Do you want to make this cake but don't have a lot of time? Try starting with a white cake mix. Prepare batter according to package directions. Mix crumbled cookies into the batter and pour batter into a pan. Add a layer of cookies in the middle of the batter. Bake the cake according to package directions.

Trusty Tip

To separate egg whites, carefully crack eggs into an egg separater. The whites will drip into the bowl, but the yolk will stay in place. Throw away yolks and shells.

23

One bite of this cake and you'll think you're on a Hawaiian beach. And because this cake is made in the microwave, you're left with more time to relax in the sun.

DIFFICULTY LEVEL: ★ ☆ ☆
MAKES: 1 (9 X 9) CAKE

MICROWAVE ALOHA CAKE

WHAT YOU NEED

●● *Ingredients*

1 ripe banana
2 eggs
¾ cup chopped macadamia nuts, (optional)
¾ cup flour
¾ cup sugar
½ teaspoon baking soda
1 teaspoon baking powder
1 teaspoon cinnamon
½ tablespoon vanilla extract
½ cup vegetable oil
½ cup crushed pineapple, undrained
½ package (4 ounces) cream cheese, softened
3 tablespoons butter, softened
⅔ cup powdered sugar
1 tablespoon crushed pineapple, undrained

●● *Tools*

mixing bowl

fork

2 small bowls

electric mixer

rubber scraper

glass pie pan

oven mitt

pot holder

1 In a mixing bowl, mash banana with a fork.

2 Crack eggs into a small bowl and throw away shells. Add eggs, ½ cup macadamia nuts, flour, sugar, baking soda, baking powder, cinnamon, vanilla, vegetable oil, and crushed pineapple to the mixing bowl. Using an electric mixer, blend on low speed for 1 minute. Mix 2 more minutes on medium speed.

3 With a rubber scraper, spread batter in a glass pie pan. Microwave for 6 minutes. If batter is still runny, microwave an additional 2–4 minutes.

4 Use oven mitts or pot holders to remove pie pan from microwave. Allow cake to cool for 1 hour.

5 In a small bowl, combine cream cheese, butter, powdered sugar, and 1 tablespoon crushed pineapple. Mix ingredients together with the fork.

6 When cake has cooled, spread frosting over the cake. Decorate cake with leftover macadamia nuts and crushed pineapple.

Aloha! Aloha! Aloha!

In the Hawaiian language, the word aloha has several different meanings. It means both hello and good-bye. It also means love.

25

For the ultimate sweet treat, this recipe is part brownie and part chocolate cake. Together, it's a winning combination.

DIFFICULTY LEVEL: ★ ★ ☆
MAKES: 1 (9 X 9) CAKE
PREHEAT OVEN: 350° FAHRENHEIT

BROWNIE LAYER CAKE

WHAT YOU NEED

•• *Ingredients*

1 cup (2 sticks) butter, melted
2 cups sugar
1 tablespoon vanilla extract
4 eggs
¾ cup cocoa powder
1 cup flour
¾ teaspoon baking powder
½ teaspoon salt
1(16-ounce) can chocolate frosting
½ cup chopped walnuts (optional)

•• *Tools*

mixing bowl   rubber scraper   2 small bowls

2 cake pans   oven mitt   pot holder

nonstick cooking spray
dinner plate

1 In a mixing bowl, combine butter, sugar, and vanilla. Mix ingredients together with a rubber scraper.

2 Crack one egg into a small bowl and throw away shell. Add egg to the mixing bowl and stir ingredients together. Repeat with the other eggs.

3 In a small bowl, mix cocoa, flour, baking powder, and salt with the rubber scraper. Add dry ingredients to the mixing bowl and stir ingredients together.

4 Spray cake pans with nonstick cooking spray. Pour half of the batter into each pan. Bake for 30 minutes or until the edges become crusty.

5 Use oven mitts or pot holders to remove the cake pans from the oven. Allow cakes to cool for 1 hour.

6 Place one cake on a dinner plate. Frost the top of the cake. Place the other cake on the frosted cake. Frost the top and sides of the cake. Sprinkle chopped walnuts on top.

Cake or Cookie?

Officially, brownies are considered bar cookies. The first recipe for chocolate brownies was published just over a century ago. No one knows for sure who invented brownies, but some people think they were invented by mistake. While baking chocolate cakes, people may have forgotten a few ingredients. They ended up with this delicious invention.

TOOLS GLOSSARY

9 x 13 baking pan — a glass or metal pan used to bake food

angel food cake pan — a round tube pan used to bake cake

baking cups — disposable paper or foil cups that are placed into a muffin pan to keep batter from sticking to the pan

baking sheet — a flat, metal tray used to bake food

Bundt pan — a round tube pan with scalloped sides used to bake cake

cake pan — a round or square pan used to bake cake

cutting board — a wooden or plastic board used when slicing or chopping foods

electric mixer — a hand-held or stand-based mixer that uses rotating beaters to mix ingredients

fork — an eating utensil often used to stir or mash

loaf pan — a rectangular-shaped pan used to bake food

microwave-safe bowl — a non-metal bowl used in microwave ovens

mixing bowl — a sturdy bowl used for mixing ingredients

muffin pan — a pan with individual cups for baking cupcakes or muffins

oven mitt — a large mitten made from heavy fabric used to protect hands when removing hot pans from the oven

paring knife — a small, sharp knife used for peeling or slicing

pastry blender — a tool used for mixing dough

pie pan — a glass or metal pan used for baking pies

pot holder — a thick, heavy fabric cut into a square or circle that is used to remove hot pans from an oven

rolling mat — a flat, plastic surface used when rolling out dough

rolling pin — a cylinder-shaped tool used to flatten dough

rubber scraper — a kitchen tool with a rubber paddle on one end

saucepan — a deep pot with a handle used for stovetop cooking

serrated knife — a kitchen knife with a saw-toothed blade used to cut

small bowl — a bowl used for mixing a small amount of ingredients

tablespoon — an eating utensil often used to stir or scoop

whisk — a metal tool used for beating ingredients

wire cooling rack — a rectangular rack that allows baked goods to cool quickly and evenly

wooden spoon — a tool made of wood with a handle on one end and bowl shaped surface on the other

GLOSSARY

centerpiece (SEN-tur-peese) — a decorative object at the center of a table

craving (KRAYV-een) — a strong desire for something

cream (KREEM) — to mix ingredients until soft and smooth

extract (EK-strakt) — a strong solution of liquid made from plant juice; vanilla extract is made from vanilla beans.

line (LINE) — to cover the inside surface

parchment (PARCH-muhnt) — a strong, heat-resistant paper used to keep food from sticking to a pan

serrated (SAR-ray-tid) — saw-toothed

tradition (truh-DISH-uhn) — a custom, idea, or belief passed down through time

READ MORE

Brenn-White, Megan. *Bake Me a Cake: Fun and Easy Treats for Kids.* Hands-Free Step-By-Step Guides. New York: HarperCollins, 2005.

Crespo, Clare. *Hey There, Cupcake!: 35 Yummy Fun Cupcake Recipes for All Occasions.* New York: Melcher Media, 2004.

Johnson, Kristi. *Monkey Pudding and Other Dessert Recipes.* Fun Food for Cool Cooks. Mankato, Minn.: Capstone Press, 2008.

INTERNET SITES

FactHound offers a safe, fun way to find Internet sites related to this book. All of the sites on FactHound have been researched by our staff.

Here's how:
1. Visit *www.facthound.com*
2. Choose your grade level.
3. Type in this book ID **1429620161** for age-appropriate sites. You may also browse subjects by clicking on letters, or by clicking on pictures and words.
4. Click on the **Fetch It** button.

FactHound will fetch the best sites for you!

ABOUT THE AUTHOR

Brekka Hervey Larrew began cooking with her mother when she was a child, mainly because she loved to eat (and still does). As a teenager, she held elaborate seven-course dinner parties for friends and relatives. Larrew baked as many varieties of cookies as she could find in recipe books. She has experimented with multicultural cooking and has spent a lot of time perfecting the art of baking pies.

Larrew taught elementary and middle school for 12 years. Currently, she stays home with her two children, both of whom help out in the kitchen. She lives in Nashville.

INDEX